THE DUA BOOK

Contains 100 everyday supplication and invocation for Muslims with transliteration and translation compiled from the both the Quran and Hadith

2

TABLE OF CONTENT

4

INTRODUCTION

In the name of Allah, the most beneficent and the most merciful. All praise and adoration is due to Allah the lord of the worlds, We give him all the praise and seek his refuge from Shaytaan the cursed one. We seek his forgiveness from the evil of our souls and wickedness of our deeds. We acknowledge that whomsoever Allah guides, none can misguides and whomsoever he misguides, none can guide. We send blessings and salutations upon the noblest of Mankind, Prophet Muhammad (pbuh), may the peace and blessings of Allah be upon him, his family, his companion and the generality of Muslims from this day until the day of resurrection. Finally we thank Allah for the blessings of Islam and for guiding us unto the right path. May he keep our faith firm on this path of Islam and grant us Paradise on the day of Judgment.

Islam as a religion is a complete way of life, every aspect of a Muslim's life is meant to conform to certain laid down principles and guidelines. One of the principles in Islam is the necessity of making dua. Dua means invocations or supplications. As Muslims we are enjoined to supplicate to Allah at every point in our lives. Allah said in the Quran Chapter 2: Verse 187 " *And when my servant ask you, [o Muhammad], concerning Me - Indeed I am near. I respond to the invocation of the supplicant when he calls upon Me, So let them respond to Me in [by obedience] and believe* in Me that they may be rightly guided". In another verse in Chapter 40: Verse 60 "And your Lord says, Call on Me; I will answer your prayers. But those who are too arrogant to worship me will surely find themselves in Hell, in humiliation". The verses above affirms the readiness of our lord to accept his servants invocations and supplication, and essentially encourages the believers to call upon him. He asks us to lay our fears, hopes, dreams before him as he will surely answer them. Dua is an expression of submission of faith to Allah and of one's need of his assistance. It serves as the weapon of the believers, as Muslims we are fortunate enough to have legislated dua from the prophet for our everyday activities, these Dua ranges from Dua for sleeping, to the one for settling debt, to the one said during Solat, all of which are forms of worship. Dua is also considered a form of worship which is a reward able act by Allah. Prophet Muhammad was reported to have said " The most excellent form of worship is dua".

Abu Sa'id al-Khudri reported: The Prophet, peace and blessings be upon him, said, *"There is no Muslim who supplicates to Allah without sin or cutting family ties in it but that Allah will give him one of three answers: he will hasten fulfillment of his supplication, he will store it for him in the Hereafter, or he will divert an evil from him similar to it."* They said, *"In that case we will ask for more."* The Prophet said, *"Allah has even more."*

13

From when a Muslim wakes up in the morning till he goes back to sleep at night, there are numerous legislated dua that should be said for various activities, this means a Muslim can be engaged in worship throughout the day, which is a potential source of uncountable rewards. It serves as a source of protection and source of reward for the one who imbibes the habit of always reciting these duas. This book highlights these supplications breaking down the necessary dua in the everyday life of a muslim. The source of the supplications are from the Quran and the hadith of prophet Muhammad(pbuh)

Etiquettes of making dua

Actions in Islam has etiquettes to go with them, supplicating and invoking the name of Allah is not an exception, the dua is more likely to be accepted by Allah if these etiquettes are followed. They include

1. Faithfulness and absolute sincerity while making the dua
2. To be clean and in the state of ablution
3. Start by thanking and praising Allah, and send blessings on Prophet Muhammad (pbuh)
4. Raising one's hand and facing the QIblah
5. Passing the hand over the face after making the dua
6. Saying Ameen after the dua
7. Trust in Allah and have the conviction that the dua would be accepted by Allah

8. Having patience and being persistent while making the dua
9. Ask Allah alone
10. Not being loud while making the dua, a moderate voice is advised
11. Not making dua against oneself, family, kin and wealth
12. Acknowledging one's sins and inadequacies and asking for forgiveness
13. Not asking for prohibited and impossible requests
14. Keeping the ties of kinship
15. Keeping Allah's injunctions and not transgressing

Special times when dua are readily accepted

There are some specific times during the day where prophet Muhammad advised us to intensify our supplications because there are special times where any supplication made is readily accepted by Allah. These special times include

1. Between the Adhan and Iqamat
2. The last third of the night
3. Throughout Fridays, the day of Jumuah
4. When it is raining
5. During Ramadan and especially the last 10 days of the month.
6. Just before breaking the fast during the month of Ramadan

7. During time of difficulty
8. After each five daily solat.
9. After reading the Quran

Special people whose dua are readily accepted

They include:

1. The dua of the righteous child for his/her parent.
2. The dua of the oppressed
3. The dua of the traveller
4. The dua of the parents upon the child

The dua of a muslim is accepted by Allah in three ways:

1. He will speedily answer him
2. He will save it for him until the Hereafter
3. He will avert something bad from him equal to the value of his du'a.

The evidence for this is in the Hadith of Abu Sa'id al-Khudr. He reported that the Prophet, peace and blessings be upon him, said, *"There is no Muslim who supplicates to Allah without sin or cutting family ties in it but that Allah will give him one of three answers: he will hasten fulfillment of his supplication, he will store it for him in the Hereafter, or he will divert an evil from him similar to it."* They said, "In that case we will ask for more." The Prophet said, *"Allah has even more."*

Chapter 1: MORNING SUPPLICATIONS AND INVOCATIONS FOR TRAVELLERS

1. Supplication for waking up:

الْحَمْدُ لِلّهِ الّذِي أَحْيَانَا بَعْدَ مَا أَمَاتَنَا وإِلَيْهِ النُّشُور

Alhamdu lillahil-ladhi ahyaana ba'ada ma amaatana wa ilaihin nushuur

Meaning: Praise be to Allah who brought us back to life after death (sleep) and to him is the return

الْحَمْدُ لِلّهِ الّذِي عَافَانِى فِي جَسَدِي و رد علَيّ روْحِي و أذن لِي بِذِكْره

Alhamdu lillahil ladhi aafani fi-jasadi wa radda alayya roohi, wa adhina li bidhikri

Meaning: Praise be to Allah, who returned my strength to my body, and returned my soul to me and allowed me to remember him

2. Supplication for entering the toilet:

بِسْمِ اللَّهِ اللَّهُمَّ إِنِّي أَعُوذ بِكَ مِنَ الْخُبْثِ
والْخَبَائِث

Bismillah allahumo inni a'udhu bika minal khubthi wal khabaa'ith, wa mina shaytaani rajeem.

Meaning: In the name of Allah, O' Allah, I seek your protection from the male and female form of unclean spirit and from the accursed devil.

3. Supplication on leaving the toilet:

غُفْرَانَكَ الْحَمْدُ لِلَّهِ الَّذِي أَذْهَبَ عَنِّي الأَذى
وَعَافَان

Ghufraanaka, alhamdulillahi ladhi adhaba a'nnil hadha wa a'nfani

Meaning: I seek your forgiveness, All praise is due to Allah, that made me leave here

4. Morning Dua for when the sun rises

أَصْبَحْنا وأَصْبَحْ المُلكُ لله رب العالَمـين ،
اللّهُمّ إِنّي أَسأَلُكَ خَيْرَ هذا اليَوْم ، فَتْحَهُ ،
ونَصْرَه ، ونُوره وبَرَكَتَهُ ، وهُداه ، وأعـوذ بِكَ
مِنْ شَرّ ما فيهِ وشَرّ ما بَعْدَه

Asbaana wa asbaha-l-mulku lillahi robbi-l- a'lameen.
Allahumo inniy asaluka khayra hadha-l-yawm, fathahu wa
nosorohu wa nuruhu wa barakatuhu wa hudahu wa
a'udhubika min sharri ma fihi wa sharri ma ba'dahu

Meaning : We are here this morning and all sovereignty
belongs to Allah, the lord of the worlds. O' Allah I am
asking you for the good present in today, its success, help,
light and blessings, and I seek refuge from the evil of the
day that is to come later.

اللّهُمّ مَا أَصْبَحَ بِي مِنْ نِعْمَةٍ أو بِأَحَدٍ مِنْ خَلْقِكَ
فَمِنْكَ وَحْدكَ لا شَريكَ لَكَ فَلَكَ الْحَمْدُ ولَكَ
الشُّكْر

Allahumo ma asbahbi min ni'matin aw bi ahdin min khalqika fa minka wahdak la shareekalak wa lakal hamdu wa laka shukru

Meaning: O Allah, whatever goodness has been for me this morning or for any of your creation is from you alone, you have no partner, All praise is unto you.

5. When undressing

بِسْمِ اللّه

Bismillahi

Meaning: In the name of Allah

6. When getting dressed

الْحَمْدُ لِلّهِ الّذِي كَسَانِي هَذَا ورزقَنيهِ مِنْ غَيْر حَوْل مِنِّي ولاَ قُوّة

Alhamdulillahi lladhi kasaanee hadha wa razaqanihi min ghayri hawli minni wala quwwat

Meaning: Praise be to Allah who has clothed and provided for me even though I was helpless and powerless.

7. When putting on new clothes

اللَّهُمّ لَكَ الْحَمْدُ كَمَا كَسَوْتَنِيهِ أَسْأَلُكَ خَيْرَه وَخَيْرَ مَا صُنِعَ لَهُ وَأَعُوذ مِنْ شَرّه وَشَرّ مَا صُنِعَ لَهُ

Allahumo laka-l- hamdu kama kasawtaneehi, as- aluka khayrahu wa khayra ma suni'a lahu wa a'udhubika min shari ma suni'a lahu

Meaning: O Allah, praise is to You. You have clothed me. I ask You for its goodness and the goodness of what it has been made for, and I seek Your protection from the evil of it and the evil of what it has been made for

8. On leaving the house

بِسْمِ اللّه تَوَكّلْت عَلَى اللّه وَلاَ حَوْل وَلاَ قُوّة إِلاّ بِاللّه

Bismillahi tawakkalitu a'la llahi wala hawla wala quwwata, illa billahi

Meaning: In the name of Allah, I put my trust in Allah, there is no power or protection except that of Allah

9. On entering the house

اللّهُمّ إِنّي أَسْأَلُكَ خَيْرَ الْمَوْلِجِ وَخَيْرَ الْمَخْرَجِ بِسْمِ اللّهِ وَلِجْنَا وَعَلَى اللّهِ رَبّنَا تَوَكّلْنَا

Allahumo inni asaluka khayra-l- mawlij wa khayra-l- makhraj, bismillahi walijna wa a'la llahi robbina tawakalna

Meaning:O our Lord, I'm asking for a good entry and exit,, In the name of Allah I enter(my house) and upon my Lord I place my trust.

10.   Supplication for mounting a vehicle

بِسْمِ اللّهِ وَالْحَمْدُ لِلّهِ، سُبْحَانَ الّذِي سَخّرَ لَنَا هَذَا وَمَا كُنّا لَهُ مُقْرِنِينَ، وَإِنّا إِلَى رَبّنَا لَمُنْقَلِبُونَ، الْحَمْدُ لِلّهِ، الْحَمْدُ لِلّهِ، الْحَمْدُ لِلّهِ، اللّهُ أَكْبَرُ، اللّهُ أَكْبَرُ، سُبْحَانَكَ

اللَّهُمَّ إِنِّي ظَلَمْتُ نَفْسِي فَاغْفِرْ لِي، فَإِنَّهُ لاَ يَغْفِرُ الذُّنُوب إِلاَّ أَنْت

Bismillahi walihamdu lillahi, subhana llahi sakharalana hadha wa ma kunna lahu mukrineen, wa inna illa robbinaa lamunqaliboon, Alhamdulillahi (x3), Allahu Akbar (x3), Subhaanaka- llahumo inny tholamtu nafsee faghfirly wala yaghfiru dhunuuba ila anta

Meaning: In the Name of Allah. Praise be to Allah. Glory is to Him Who has provided this for us though we could never have had it by our efforts. Surely, unto our Lord we are returning. Praise is to Allah. Praise is to Allah. Praise is to Allah. Allah is the Most Great. Allah is the Most Great. Allah is the Most Great. Glory is to You. O Allah, I have wronged my own soul. Forgive me, for surely none forgives sins but You.

11.   Supplication for traveling

اللهُ أَكبَرَ ، اللهُ أَكبَرَ ، اللهُ أَكبَرَ، سُبْحان الَّذي سَخَّرَ لَنا هذا وَما كُنّا لَهُ مُقْرنين، وإنّا إلى رَبِّنا لَمُنْقَلِبون، اللّهُمَّ إنّا نَسْأَلُكَ في

سَفَرِنا هذا البِرّ والتّقْوى، وَمِنَ الْعَمَلِ ما
تَرْضى، اللّهُمّ هَوّنْ عَلَينا سَفَرَنا هذا واطْوِ
عَنّا بُعْدَه، اللّهُمّ أَنْتَ الصّاحِبُ في
السّفَرِ، والْخَلِيفَةُ في الأهلِ، اللّهُمّ إِنّي
أَعوذُبِكَ مِنْ وَعْثاءِ السّفَرِ، وكآبَةِ الْمَنْظَرِ،
وَسوءِ الْمُنْقَلَبِ في المالِ والأَهْلِ

Allaahu 'Akbar, Allaahu 'Akbar, Allaahu 'Akbar, Subhaanal-ladhee sakhkhara lanaa haadhaa wa maa kunnaa lahu muqrineen. Wa innaa ilaa Robbinaa lamunqaliboon. Allaahumma innaa nas'aluka fee safarinaa haadhal-birrawattaqwaa, waminal-'amalimaa tardoo, Allaahumma hawwin 'alaynaa safaranaa haadhaa watwi 'annaa bu'dahu, Allaahumma Antas-saahibu fis-safari, walkhaleefatu fil-ahli, Allaahumma innee a'oothu bika min wa'thaa'is-safari, wa ka'aabatil-manthari, wa soo'il-munqalabi fil-maaliwal'ahli).

Meaning: Allah is the Most Great. Allah is the Most Great. Allah is the Most Great. Glory is to Him Who has provided this for us though we could never have had it by our efforts. Surely, unto our Lord we are returning. O Allah, we ask you on this our journey for goodness and piety, and for works that are pleasing to you. O Allah , lighten this journey for us and make its distance easy for us. O Allah, You are our companion on the road and the one in whose care we leave our family. O Allah, I seek refuge in you from this journey's hardships, and from the wicked sights in store and from finding our family and property in misfortune upon returning.

12.　　Supplication upon entering a town

أللَّهُمّ رب السَّمَوَات السّبْعِ وَمَا أَظْلَلْنَ، ورب الأَراضِينَ السّبْعِ وَما أَقْلَلْنَ، ورب الشّيَاطِينِ وَمَا أَضْلَلْنَ، ورب الرِّيَاح وَمَا ذرِيْنَ، أَسأَلُكَ خَيْرَ هَذِهِ الْقَرْيَةِ وَخَيْرَ أَهلِهَا، وَخَيْرَ مَا فِيهَا، وأَعُوذ بِكَ مِنْ شَرِّهَا، وَشَرّ أَهلِهَا، وشَرّ مَا فِيهَا

Allahumo rabbas-samawaati sab'i wa maa athlalna wa rabal-araadeena sab'i wa maa aqlalna wa rabbas-shayaateen wa maa adlalna wa rabbar- riyaahi wa maa dharayna, as-aluka khayra hadhihil- qaryati wa khayra ahlihaa wa khayra maa fiihaa wa a'udhubika min sharrihaa wa sharri ahlihaa wa sharri maa fiihaa

Meaning: O Allah, Lord of the Seven heavens and all they overshadow, Lord of the Seven worlds and all they uphold, Lord of the devils and all they lead astray, Lord of the winds and all they scatter. I ask You for the goodness of this town and for the goodness of its people, and for the goodness it contains. I seek refuge in You from its evil, from the evil of its people and from the evil it contains

13.   Supplication On entering a market

لاَ إِلَهَ إِلاَّ اللَّهُ وَحْدَهُ لاَ شَرِيكَ لَهُ، لَهُ الْمُلْكُ وَلَهُ الْحَمْدُ، يُحْيِي وَيُمِيتُ وَهُوَ حَيٌّ لاَ يَمُوتُ، بِيَدِهِ الْخَيْرُ وَهُوَ عَلَى كُلِّ شَيْءٍ قَدِيرٍ

Laillaha illalahu wahdahu laa shareekalka- lahu lahul- mulku wa lahul- hamdu yuhyi wa yumeetu wa huwa hayyu laa yamuut biyadihil- khayru wa huwa a'la kulli shayin qadeer

Meaning: There is no god but Allah alone, Who has no partner. His is the dominion and His is the praise. He brings life and He causes death, and He is living and does not die. In His Hand is all good, and He is Able to do all things.

14. When the means of transport stumbles

بِسْمِ اللّٰه

Bismillahi

Meaning: In the name of Allah

15. Supplication of the one visitor for the host

أَسْتَوْدِعُكُمُ اللّٰهَ الَّذِي لاَ تَضِيعُ ودائِعُه

Astawdi'uka - llahi ladhi laa tadee'u wa daa-hi'uhu

Meaning: I leave you in the care of Allah, as nothing is lost that is in His care.

16. Supplication of the host for the visitor

أَسْتَوْدع اللّٰهَ دِينَكَ، وأمَانَتَكَ، وَخَوَاتِيمَ عَمَلِك

Astawdi'uka llahi deeneka wa amaanataka wa khawaateema a'malika

Meaning: I leave your religion in the care of Allah, as well as your safety, and the last of your deeds.

17. Supplication for the traveler as dawn approaches

سَمِعَ سَامِعُ بِحَمْدِ اللَّهِ، وَحُسْنِ بَلَائِهِ عَلَيْنَا.

رَبَّنَا صَاحِبْنَا وَأَفْضِلْ عَلَيْنَا عَائِذًا بِاللَّهِ مِنَ

النَّار

Samia' saamiu' bihamdillahi wa husni balaa-ihi a'layna. Rabbana soohibana wa afdil a'laynaa a'a-hidhan billahi mina- naar

Meaning: He Who listens has heard that we praise Allah for the good things He gives us. Our Lord, be with us and bestow Your favor upon us. I seek the protection of Allah from the Fire.

CHAPTER 2   DUA DURING ABLUTION AND SOLAT

18.   At the start of ablution

بِسْمِ اللّه

Bismillahi

Meaning: In the name of Allah

19.   After the ablution

أَشْهَدُ أن لاَ إِلَهَ إلاّ الله وَحْدَهُ لاَ شَرِيكَ لَهُ،
وأَشْهَدُ أَن مُحَمَّدا عَبْدُهُ ورَسُوُلُه

Ashadu an la illaha illallahu wahdahu la shareekalahu, wa ashadu Anna Muhammadan a'bduhu wa rosuluhu

Meaning: I bear witness that there is no god but Allah, he is one and has no partner, and I bear witness that Muhammad is his slave and messenger.

اللّهُمّ اجْعَلْنِي مِنَ التّوابِين واجْعَلْنِي مِن
الْمُتَطَهِّرين

Allahumo ij'alni Mina tawwabin waj'alni Minna-l-mutatohirrin

Meaning: O' Allah make me amongst those who repent and those who stay pure

20. When entering the Mosque

السَّلَام عَلَيْكُمْ ورحْمَةُ اللهِ وبَرَكَاتُه

As salamu alaykum warahmatullah wabarakatuh

Meaning: May the peace and blessings of Allah be upon you

رب اغْفِرْ لِي ذُنُوبِي وافْتَحْ لِي أَبْواب رَحْمَتِك

Robbi ighfirly dhunuby waftahly abwaaba rahmatik

Meaning: O my lord grant me forgiveness for my sins and open the doors of mercy for me

21.   On hearing the adhan:

أَشْهَدُ أَن لاَ إِلَهَ إِلاّ اللّهُ وَحْدَهُ لاَ شَرِيكَ لَهُ
وَأَشْهَدُ أَن مُحَمَّدَا عَبْدَه وَرَسُولَهُ وَأَشْهَدُ
أَن مُحَمَّدَا عَبْدَه وَرَسُولَهُ رَضِيتُ بِاللّهِ رَبَّاً
وَبِمُحَمَّدٍ رَسُولاً وَبِالإِسْلاَم دِينَا

Ashadu an la illaha illallahu wahdahu la shareekalahu, wa ashadu Anna Muhammadan a'bduhu wa rosuluhu, rodeetu billahi rabba wa bil islami deena, wabi Muhammad in nabiyyan wa rosullah

Meaning: I bear witness that there is no god but Allah, he is one and has no partner, and I bear witness that Muhammad is his slave and messenger. I am pleased with Allah as my lord, with Islam as my religion and with prophet Muhammad as my messenger.

22. When standing up for solat

سُبْحَانَكَ اللَّهُمَّ وَبِحَمْدِكَ، وَتَبَارك

اسْمُكَ، وَتَعَالَى جَدُّك وَلاَ إِلَهَ غَيْرُك

Subhaanaka Allaahumma wa bihamdika, wa tabaarakasmuka, wa ta'aalaa jadduka, wa laa 'ilaaha ghayruka

Meaning: All glory and praise is to you Allah, blessed is your name and exalted is your majesty, and there is no god except you.

23. While bowing down (Rukooh)

سُبْحَان رَبِّي الْعَظِيمِ فغْفِرْ لِي

Subhaanaka robiyyal a'zeem faghfirly (Thrice)

Meaning: Glory be to my lord the exalted one, Forgive me

سُبُّوحٌ، قُدُّوسٌ، رب المَلاَئِكَةِ وَالرُّوح

Subuhu quddus robbi-l- malaaikati wa rruhu

Meaning: Glory belongs to you, the most Holy one, lord of all the angels and the spirit (Jubreel)

24. On rising from the Rukooh position (Bowing down)

سَمِعَ اللّهَ ُلِمَـنْ حَمِدَه

Sam'i Allahu liman Hamida

Meaning: Allah hears those who praise him

رَبّنَا وَلَكَ الْحَمْدْ، حَمْدا كَثِيرا طَيِّباً مُبَاركاً فِيه

Rabbana walaka-l-hamdu, hamdan katheeran, toyyiban, mubaarakan fihi

Meaning: All praise is yours our Lord, abundant, pure and blessed praises.

25. During prostration (Sujood)

سُبْحَان رَبِّي َالأَعْلَى فغْفِرْ لِي

Subhanaka robbiyal a'ala faghfirly (Thrice)

Meaning: Glory be to my Lord the most high, forgive me

سُبُّوحْ، قُدُّسْ، رب الْمَلاَئِكَةِ والرُّوح

Subuhu quddus robbi-l- malaaikati wa rruhu

Meaning: Glory belongs to you, the most Holy one, lord of all the angels and the spirit (Jubreel)

26.   Between the two prostration

رب اغْفِرْ لِي   رب اغْفِرْ لِي

Robbi ighfirly, Robbi ighfirly

Meaning: Lord forgive me, Lord forgive me

27.   The tashahud

التّحِيّات لِلّهِ، والصّلَوَاتُ، والطّيّبَاتُ، السّلَامُ
عَلَيكَ أَيّهَا النّبِيّ ورَحْمَةُ اللّهِ وبَرَكَاتُهُ،
السّلَامُ عَلَيْنَا وعَلَى عِبَاد لله الصّالِحِينَ.
أَشْهَدُ أَن لاَ إِلَهَ إِلاّ اللّهَ، وأَشهدُ أَن مُحَمّدا
عَبْدُهُ ورسُولُهُ

Attahiyatu lillahi, wasalawatu wa toyyibat, Assalamu alayka ayyhua nabiyyu, wa rahmotullahi wabarakatuh, Assalamu alayka wa a'la i'baadi llahi soliheen, ashadu an La illaha illallahu, wa ashadu anna Muhammadan a'bduhu wa rosuluhu

Meaning: All greetings of humility are for Allah, and all prayers and all things pure, Peace be upon you, O Prophet, and the mercy of Allah and His blessings. Peace be upon us and upon the righteous slaves of Allah. I bear witness that there is no god but Allah, and I bear witness that prophet Muhammad is His slave and His Messenger.

28.   Prayer upon the prophet after the tashahud:

اللَّهُمَّ صَلِّ عَلَى مُحَمَّدٍ وَعَلَى آلِ مُحَمَّدٍ، كَمَا صَلَّيْتَ عَلَى إِبْرَاهِيمَ وَعَلَى آلِ إِبْرَاهِيمَ، إِنَّكَ حَمِيدٌ مَجِيدٌ، اللَّهُمَّ بَارِك عَلَى مُحَمَّدٍ وَعَلَى آلِ مُحَمَّدٍ، كَمَا بَارَكْتَ عَلَى إِبْرَاهِيمَ وَعَلَى آلِ إِبْرَاهِيمَ، إِنَّكَ حَمِيدٌ مَجِيدٌ

Allahumo solli a'la Muhammad wa a'la ahli Muhammad, kama solayta a'la ibroheem wa a'la ahli ibroheem innaka hamidun mojeed, allahumo bariki Lana Muhammad wa a'la ahli Muhammad, kama baarakta a'la ibroheem wa a'la ahli ibroheem, innaka hamidun mojeed

Meaning: O our lord send your blessings on Muhammad and his household just as you sent your blessings on Ibroheem and his household, verily you are worthy of all praise and most glorious, O our lord bless Muhammad and his household, just as you blessed Ibroheem and his household, verily you are worthy of all praises and most glorious.

29.   Other supplications after the tashahud before final tasleem

اللّهُمّ إِنّي أَعُوذ بِكَ مِنْ عَذَابِ القَبْرِ، وَمِنْ عَذَابِ جَهَنّمَ، وَمِن فِتْنَةِ الْمَحْيَا والْمَمَاتِ، وَمِنْ شَرّ فِتْنَةِ الْمَسِيحِ الدّجّال

Allahumo inni a'udhubika Min a'dhabil qabri wa min a'dhabi jahannam, wa min fitnatil mahya Wal mamaat wa min sharri fitnatil maseehu dajjal

Meaning: O our lord, we seek refuge from the punishment of the grave, and the punishment of hell fire, and the problems in life and death and from the problem of the false Messiah

اللّهُمّ إِنِّي ظَلَمْتُ نَفْسِي ظُلْماً كَثِيرا وَلاَ يَغْفِرُ الذُّنُوب إِلاّ أَنْتَ، فَاغْفِرْ لِي مَغْفِرَة مِنْ عِنْدِك وارْحَمْنِي، إِنّك أَنْتَ الْغَفُور الرّحِيم

Allahumo inni thalamtu nafsee thulman katheeran, walaa yaghfiru dhunuba illa anta, faghfirly maghfiratan min i'ndika, warhamni innaka anta-l- ghafuru raheem

Meaning: O our Lord, I have wronged my soul greatly, no one forgives sins but you, please forgive me and have mercy on me. Verily you are the forgiver and the most merciful.

اللّهُمّ إِنِّي أَسْأَلُك الْجَنّةَ وأَعُوذ بِك مِنَ النّار

Allahumo inni as-aluka-l- Janna wa a'udhubika Minna maar.

Meaning: O our Lord , grant me paradise and protect me from hell fire

30. Recommended supplications after solat

أَسْتَغْفِرُ اللّهَ   (ثَلَاث)ا

Astaghfirullahi (Thrice)

Meaning: O Allah forgive me

اللّهُمّ أَنْتَ السّلَامُ، وَمِنْكَ السّلَامُ، تَبَارَكْتَ يَا ذَا الْجَلَال والإكْرَام

Allahumo anta salaam wa minka salaam, tabaarakta yaa dhaljalaali wali ikraam

Meaning: O Allah you are peace and peace is from you, blessed is your name, the owner of Majesty and Honor

لَا إِلَهَ إِلّا اللّهَ وَحْدَه وَحْدَه لاَ شَرِيك لَهُ، لَهُ الْمُلْكُ وَلَهُ الْحَمْدُ وَهُوَ عَلَى كُلِ شَيْء قَدِيرٍ، اللّهُمّ

لَا مَانِعَ لِمَا أَعْطَيْتَ، ولا مُعْطِيَ لِمَا مَنَعْتَ، ولَا يَنْفَعُ ذا الْجَدِّ مِنك الْجَد.

La illaha illallahu wahdahu la shareekalak lahul Mulki walahu-l- hamdu, wa huwa a'la kulli shayin qadeer. Allahumo la maan'i limaa a'atayta wa laa mu'ti Lima mana'at wa la yanfa'u dhal jaddi minka-l- jaddu

Meaning: There is no god but you Allah, He is one and has no partner, he has dominion over all things and all praise is due to him and he is able to do all things. O Allah there is no one who can hold back what you've given and there is no one who can give out what you hold back, and the might of the mighty person cannot benefit him against you.

لَا إِلَهَ إِلَّا اللَّهُ وَحْدَهُ وَحْدَهُ لَا شَرِيك لَهُ، لَهُ الْمُلْك

وَلَهُ الْحَمْدُ وَهُوَ عَلَى كُلِّ شَيْءٍ قَدِيرٌ، لَا

حَوْل ولَا قُوَّة إِلَّا بِاللَّهِ، لَا إِلَهَ إِلَّا اللَّهِ، وَلَا

نَعْبُدُ إِلَّا إِيَّاهُ، لَهُ النِّعْمَةُ وَلَهُ الْفَضْلُ وَلَهُ

الثَّنَاء الْحَسَنِ، لَا إِلَهَ إِلاّ اللّه مُخْلِصِينَ لَهُ
الدِّينَ وَلَوْ كَرِه الْكَافِرُون

Laa 'ilaaha 'illallaahu, wa laa na'budu 'illaa 'iyyaahu, lahun-ni'mat wa lahul-fadhlu wa lahuth-thanaa'ul-hasanu, laa 'ilaaha 'illallaahu mukhliseena lahud-deena wa law karihal-kaafiroon.

Meaning: There is no god but Allah, and we do not worship anyone but you, For him is goodness, bounty and the best of praises. There is no god but Allah, we are sincere in our religion even though the disbelievers hate it.

سُبْحَان اللّه   (ثلاثاً وثلاثين)ن

الْحَمْدُ لِلّه   (ثلاثاً وثلاثين)ن

اللّه أَكْبَرُ   (ثلاثاً وثلاثين)ن

Subhanallahi (thirty three times)

Alhamdulillahi (thirty three times)

Allahu Akbar (thirty three times)

Meaning:

All glory belong to Allah

All praises belong to Allah

Allah is great

لَا إِلَهَ إِلَّا اللَّهُ وَحْدَهُ وَحْدَهُ لاَ شَرِيكَ لَهُ، لَهُ الْمُلْكُ

وَلَهُ الْحَمْدُ وَهُوَ عَلَى كُلِّ شَيْءٍ قَدِير

La ilaaha 'illallaahu wahdahu laa shareeka lahu, lahul-mulku wa lahul-hamdu wa Huwa'alaa kulli shay'in qadeer

Meaning: There is no god but Allah, He is one and has no partner, he has dominion over all things and all praise is due to him and he is able to do all things.

31.   Aayatal kursiyy (Suratul Baqarah: Verse 225)

ٱللَّهُ لَآ إِلَهَ إِلَّا هُوَ ٱلْحَىُّ ٱلْقَيُّوم لاَ تَأْخُذُهُ

سِنَةٌ وَلاَ نَوْم لَّهُ مَا فِى ٱلسَّمَـٰوَت وَمَا فِى

ٱلْأَرْض مَن ذَا ٱلَّذِى يَشْفَعُ عِندَهُ إِلاَّ بِإِذْنِهِ

41

يَعْلَمُ مَا بَيْنَ أَيْدِيهِمْ وَمَا خَلْفَهُمْ وَلَا
يُحِيطُونَ بِشَيْءٍ مِنْ عِلْمِهِ إِلاَّ بِمَا شَآءَ وَسِعَ
كُرْسِيُّهُ ٱلسَّمَٰوَٰتِ وَٱلْأَرْضَ وَلَا يَؤُودُهُ
حِفْظُهُمَا وَهُوَ ٱلْعَلِىُّ ٱلْعَظِيمُ

Allaahu laa 'ilaaha 'illaa Huwal-Hayyul-Qayyuum, laa ta'khuthuhu sinatunw-wa laa nawm, lahu maa fis-samaawaati wa maafil- ardi, man thal-lathee yashfa'u 'indahu 'illaa bi'idhnihi, ya'alamu maa bayna 'aydeehim wa maa khalfahum, wa laa yuheetoona bishay'im-min 'ilmihi 'illaa bimaa shaa'a, wasi'a kursiyyuhus-samaawaati wal'ardh, wa laa ya'ooduhu hifdhuhumaa, wa Huwal-'Aliyyul- 'Adheem.

Meaning: O' Allah - there is no deity except Him, the Ever-Living, the Sustainer of [all] existence. Neither drowsiness overtakes Him nor sleep. To Him belongs whatever is in the heavens and whatever is on the earth. Who is it that can intercede with Him except by His permission? He knows what is [presently] before them and what will be after them, and they encompass not a thing of His knowledge except for what He wills. His Kursi extends over the heavens and the earth, and their preservation tires Him not. And He is the Most High, the Most Great.

32.   Suratul Ikhlas

بِسْمِ اللّهِ الرّحْمَـٰنِ الرّحِيم

قُلْ هُوَ اللّهُ أَحَدٌ، اللّهُ الصّمَدُ، لَمْ يَلِدْ وَلَمْ يُولَدْ، وَلَمْ يَكُنْ لّهُ كُفُوًا أَحَد.

Bismi Allahi arrahmani arraheem. Qul huwa Allahu ahad, Allahu assamad, Lam yalid walam yoolad, Walam yakun lahu kufuwan ahad.

Meaning: In the name of Allah the most beneficient, the most merciful.Say 'He is Allah, who is one. Allah, the eternal refuge. He neither begets nor is born. Nor is there to him any equivalent

33.   Suratul Falaq

بِسْمِ اللّهِ الرّحْمَـٰنِ الرّحِيم

قُلْ أَعُوذ بِرَبِّ الْفَلَقِ، مِن شَرّ مَا خَلَقَ، وَمِن شَرّ غَاسِقٍ إِذا وَقَبَ، وَمِن شَرّ النَّفَّاثَاتِ فِي الْعُقَدِ، وَمِن شَرّ حَاسِدٍ إِذا حَسَد

Bismillahi arrahmani arraheem. Qul a'aoothu birabbi alfalaq, Min sharri ma khalaq, Wamin sharri ghasiqin ithawaqab, Wamin sharri annaffathatifee al'uqad, Wamin sharri hasidin itha hasad

Meaning: In the name of Allah the most beneficient, the most merciful

Say ' I seek refuge in the lord of the day break. From the evil of that which he created. And from the evil of darkness when it settles. And from the evil of the blower in knots. And from the evil of the envier when he envies.

34.   Suratul Nas

بِسْمِ اللَّهِ الرّحْمَـٰنِ الرّحِيم

قُلْ أَعُوذ بِرَبِّ النَّاسِ، مَلِكِ النَّاسِ، إِلَـٰهِ النَّاسِ، مِن شَرّ الْوَسْوَاسِ الْخَنَّاسِ، الّذِي

يُوَسْوِسُ فِي صُدُورِ النَّاسِ، مِنَ الْجِنَّةِ وَالنَّاسِ.

Bismi Allahi arrahmani arraheem. Qul a'aoothu birabbi annas, Maliki annas, Ilahi annas, Min sharri alwaswasi alkhannas, Allathee yuwaswisu fee sudoori annas, Mina aljinnati wannas.

Meaning: In the name of Allah the most beneficient, the most merciful

Say ' I seek refuge in the Lord of mankind. The Sovereign of mankind. The God of mankind. From the evil of the retreating whisperer. Who whispers evil into the breast of mankind. From amongst the Jinn and mankind.

CHAPTER 3 SUPPLICATIONS AND INVOCATIONS DURING FASTING PERIOD

35. When the crescent moon is sighted for Ramadan

اللّهُ أَكْبَرُ، اللّهُمّ أَهِلّهُ عَلَيْنَا بِالأَمْنِ والإِيمَانِ،
والسّلامَةِ والإِسْلامِ، والتّوْفيقِ لِمَا تُحِبُّ رَبّنَا
وتَرْضَى، رَبّنَا وربُّكَ اللّه

Allahu Akbar, Allahumo ahillahu a' layna bilamni wali-eeman was-salaamatu wali Islam, wa tawfeeki Lima tuhibu rabbana wa tardaa, rabbuna wa rabbaka-llahu

Meaning: Allah is great, O Allah bring the new moon to us in security and faith, with peace and in the religion of Islam and in unity with what our Lord loves and pleases him. Our Lord and your Lord is Allah.

36. Before eating Sahur

بِسْمِ اللّه

Bismillahi

Meaning: In the name of Allah

37.   After eating Sahur

الْحَمْدُ لِلَّهِ الَّذِي أَطْعَمَنِي هَذَا الطَّعَام

ورزقَنِيهِ مِنْ غَيْرِ حَوْلٍ مِنِّي ولَا قُوَّة

Alhamdulillahi ladhi at'aamani hadhaa, wa razaqanihi Min ghayri hawli minni wala quwwat.

Meaning: All thanks is due to Allah, that fed me with this and provided for me even though I was not able to do it and lacked power.

38.   When breaking one's fast

ذَهَبَ الظَّمَأُ وابْتَلَّتِ الْعُرُوقِ، وَثَبَتَ الأَجْرُ

إن شَاء اللَّه

Dhahaba thama-u wabtalati-l- u' ruuk, wathabata-l- ajru Insha Allah

Meaning: The thirst is gone and the veins are moistened and the reward is certain of Allah wills.

اللَّهُمَّ لَكَ صُمْتُ وَعَلَى رِزْقِكَ أَفْطَرْتْ

Allahumo laka sumtu wa a'la rizqika aftortu

Meaning: O' Allah, , I have fasted for You and from the sustenance given by You, I break the fast

39.　When breaking one's fast in someone's home

أَفْطَرَ عِنْدَكُمْ الصَّائِمُونَ، وأَكَلَ طَعَامكُمُ الْأَبْرَارُ، وَصَلَّتْ عَلَيْكُمْ الْمَلائِكَة

Aftara 'indakumus-saa'imoona, wa 'akala ta'amakumul-'abraaru , wa sallat 'alaykumul-malaa'ikatu

Meaning: With you, those who are fasting have broken their fast, you have given food to the righteous and the angels are with you.

40.　When insulted while fasting

إِنِّي صَائِمٌ، إِنِّي صَائِم

Inni sooimun inni sooimun

Meaning: I am fasting, I am fasting

41. Qunut for Witr Prayer

اللّهُمَّ اهْدِنِي فِيمَنْ هَدَيْتَ، وَعَافِنِي فِيمَنْ عَافَيْتَ، وَتَوَلَّنِي فِيمَنْ تَوَلَّيْتَ، وَبَارِكْ لِي فِيمَا أَعْطَيْتَ، وَقِنِي شَرَّ مَا قَضَيْتَ، فَإِنَّكَ تَقْضِي وَلاَ يُقْضَ عَلَيْكَ، إِنَّهُ لاَ يَذِلُ مَنْ وَالَيْتَ، [وَلاَ يَعِزُّ مَنْ عَادَيْتَ]، تَبَارَكْتَ رَبِّ وَتَعَالَيْتَ

Allaahum-mahdiney feeman hadayta, wa 'aafiney feeman 'aafayta, wa tawallanee feeman tawallayta, wa baarik lee feemaa 'a'atayta, wa qinee sharra maa qadhayta, fa'innaka taqdhee wa laa yuqdhaa 'alayka, 'innahu laa yadhillu man waalayta, wa laa ya'izzu man 'aadayta, tabaarakta Rabbanaa wa ta'aalayta

O Allah, guide me with those whom You have guided, and strengthen me with those whom you have strengthened . Care for me with those who you have cared for. Bless me in what you have given me. Guard me from the evil You have ordained. Surely, You command and are not commanded, and none whom You have committed to Your care shall be humiliated (and none whom You have taken as an enemy shall taste glory). You are Blessed, Our Lord, and Exalted.

اللّهُمَّ إِنِّي أَعُوذ بِرِضَاك مِنْ سَخَطِكَ، وَبِمُعَافَاتِكَ مِنْ عُقُوبَتِكَ، وأَعُوذُ بِك مِنْك، لاَ أُحْصِي ثَنَاء عَلَيْك، أَنْت كَمَا أَثْنَيْت عَلَى نَفْسِكَ

Allaahumma 'innee 'a'uthu biridhaaka min sakhatika, wa bimu'aafaatika min 'uqubatika, wa 'a'oothu bika minka, laa 'uhsee dhanaa'an 'alayka, 'Anta kamaa 'athnayta 'alaa nafsika.

Meaning: O Allah, I seek refuge with Your Pleasure from Your anger. I seek refuge in Your forgiveness from Your punishment. I seek refuge in You from You. I cannot count Your praises, You are as You have praised Yourself

اللّهُمّ إِيّاك نَعْبُدُ، وَلَك نُصَلِّي وَنَسْجُدُ،
وَإِلَيْك نَسْعَى وَنَحْفِدُ، نَرْجُو رَحْمَتَك،
وَنَخْشَى عَذَابَك، إِن عَذَابَك بِالْكَافِرِينَ
مُلْحَقُ. اللّهُمّ إِنّا نَسْتَعِينُك، وَنَسْتَغْفِرُك،
وَنُثْنِي عَلَيْك الْخَيْرَ، وَلَا نَكْفُرُك، وَنُؤْمِنُ بِك،
وَنَخْضَعُ لَك، وَنَخْلَعُ مَنْ يَكْفُرُك

Allaahumma 'iyyaaka na'budu, wa laka nusollee wa
nasjudu, wa ilayka nas'aa wa nahfidu, narju rahmataka,
wanakhshaa 'adhaabaka, 'inna 'adhaabaka bilkaafireena
mulhaq. Allaahumma 'innaa nasta'eenuka, wa
nastaghfiruka, wa nuthnee 'alaykal-khayr, wa laa
nakfuruka, wa nu'minu bika, wa nakhda'u laka, wa
nakhla'u man yakfuruka

Meaning: O Allah, You alone do we worship and to You
we pray and prostrate to. To You we quicken to worship
and to serve. Our hope is for Your mercy and we fear Your
punishment. Surely, Your punishment of the disbelievers
is at hand. O Allah, we pray for Your help and Your

forgiveness, and we praise You beneficently. We do not deny You and we believe in You. We surrender to You and renounce whoever disbelieves in You.

42. Supplication for the last 10 days in Ramadan

اللّهُمّ اِنّكَ عَفُوٌّ تُحِبُّ الْعَفْوَ فَاعْفُ عَنِّي

Allahumo innaka a'fuwwun tuhibul- a'fuwa fa'fu- a'nni

Meaning: O' Allah you are oft-forgiving, you love to forgive so forgive me

CHAPTER 5: SUPPLICATIONS AND INVOCATIONS DURING HAJJ AND UMRAH

43. On arrival for Hajj or Umrah

لَبَّيْكَ اللَّهُمَّ لَبَّيْكَ، لَبَّيْكَ لاَ شَرِيكَ لَكَ لَبَّيْكَ،
إِنَّ الْحَمْدَ وَالنِّعْمَةَ، لَكَ وَالْمُلْكَ، لاَ شَرِيكَ
لَكَ

Labaika- llahumo labik, labaika la shareekalak labaika, innali-hamda wa n'imata lala walmulku laa shareekalak.

Meaning: I am here at your service, O Allah, I am here at your service. I am here at your service you have no partner, verily all praise, adoration and blessings is yours, you are the dominion and have no partner.

44. Supplication while making Tawaaf

سُبْحَان اللّه وَالْحَمْدُ لِلّه وَلاَ إِلَهَ إِلاَّ اللّهُ
وَاللّهُ أَكْبَرُ وَلاَ حَوْلَ وَلاَ قُوَّة إِلاَّ بِاللّه

Subhaanallahi walhamdu lillahu wa laa illaha illalahu wallahu akbar, wa la hawla wala quwwata illa billahi

Meaning: Glory be to Allah, all praise is for Allah, there is no god but Allah. He is the greatest and the one who

45. On passing the black stone

وَاللَّهُ أَكْبَر

Allahu Akbar

Meaning: Allah is great

46. When between the Yemeni corner and black stone

رَبَّنَا آتِنَا فِي الدُّنْيَا حَسَنَةً وَفِي الأَخِرَةَ حَسَنَةً

وَقِنَا عَذَابَ النّار

Robbana aatina fi Sunita hasanatan, wa fil aakhirati hasanatan wa qinaa a'dhaaban-naar

Meaning: O our Lord, grant us goodness in this life and the hereafter and protect us from hell

47. At mount safaa and Marwa
On approaching mount safaa, Say

إِنَّ الصَّفَا وَالْمَرْوَةَ مِنْ شَعَآئِرِ اللّهِ أَبْدَأُ بِمَا بَدَأَ اللّهُ بِهِ

Inna safaa Wal marwata min sha'aira llahi abadaambima bada-allahu bihi

Meaning: Verily Safaa and Marwa are amongst the sign of Allah, I start by that which Allah began.

Then say:

اللّهُ أَكْبَرُ، اللّهُ أَكْبَرُ، اللّهُ أَكْبَرُ لَا إِلَهَ إِلاَّ اللّهُ وَحْدَهُ لَا شَرِيكَ لَهُ، لَهُ الْمُلْكُ وَلَهُ الْحَمْدُ وَهُوَ عَلَى كُلِّ شَيْءٍ قَدِيرٌ، لَا إِلَهَ إِلاَّ اللّهُ وَحْدَهُ، أَنْجَزَ وَعْدَهُ، وَنَصَرَ عَبْدَهُ، وَهَزَمَ الْأَحْزَابَ وَحْدَهُ

Allahu Akbar, Allahu Akbar, Allahu Akbar, la illaha illa Allahu wahdahu laa shareekalak lahul mulku walahu-l-hamdu wahuwa a'la Mulki shayin qadeer,lanillaha illallahu anjaza wahdahu, wa nadhara a'bda wa hazama-l- ahzaab wahdahu

Meaning: Allah is great, Allah is great, Allah is great, there is no god but Allah, He is one and has no partner, for him is dominion and praise and he has power over everything. There is no god but Allah, He fulfilled his promise, helped his slaves and defeated the confederates.

48. Supplication on the day of Arafah

لاَ إِلَهَ إِلاَّ اللّهُ وَحْدَه لاَ شَرِيكَ لَه، لَه الْمُلْكُ وَلَه الْحَمْدُ وَهُوَ عَلَى كُلِّ شَيْءٍ قَدِير

La illaha illa Allahu wahdahu laa shareekalak lahul mulku walahu-l- hamdu wahuwa a'la Mulki shayin qadeer

Meaning: There is no god but Allah, He is one and has no partner, for him is dominion and praise and he has power over everything.

49. Remembrance at Muzdalifah:

اللّهُ أَكْبَر

لاَ إِلَهَ إِلاَّ اللّهُ وَحْدَه

Allahu Akbar,la illaha illallahu wahdahu

Meaning: Allah is great, there is no god but Allah and he is one.

50.   While throwing each stone at Jamaarat

اللّهُ أَكْبَر

Allahu Akbar

Allah is great.

51.   When slaughtering or offering a sacrifice

بِسْمِ اللّهِ واللّه أَكْبَرُ اللّهُمّ مِنْكَ ولَكَ اللّهُمّ تَقبّلْ مِنِي

Bismillahi, Allahu Akbar Allahumo minka walaka Allahumo taqabbal minni

Meaning: In the name of Allah, Allah is great, O Allah this is from you and to you, accept it from me

CHAPTER 5: SUPPLICATIONS FOR CALAMITY, DEBT, SICKNESS AND DFATH

52.   On visiting the sick

لاَ بَأْس طَهُور إن شَاء اللّه

La ba-asa tohuur inshallahu

Meaning: No worries, it will be a source of purification for you if Allah wills

أسأَل اللّهَ الْعَظِيمَ، رب الْعَرْش الْعَظِيمِ أن يَشْفِيَك

As-alullaha-l- atheem, rabba-l- a'rshil atheem

Meaning: I ask Almighty Allah, Lord of the Magnificent Throne, to make you well.

53.   For the terminally ill

اللّهُمّ اغْفِرْ لِي وارْحَمْنِي وألْحِقْنِي بِالرَّفِيقِ الأعْلَى

Allahumo ighfirliy wa rhamniy wa alhiqniy bir-rafeeqil a'alaa

58

Meaning: O Allah, forgive me and have mercy upon me and join me with the highest companions

لَا إِلَهَ إِلَّا اللّه إِن لِلمَوْت لَسَكَرَات

La illaha illalahu inna limawti sakharaat

Meaning: There is no god but Allah, surely death has agonies

54.   **For the one nearing death**

لَا إِلَهَ إِلَّا اللّه

La illaha illallahu

There is no god but Allah

55.   **For the one hit by a calamity**

اللّهُمّ رَحْمَتَكَ أرْجُو فَلَا تَكِلْنِي إِلَى نَفْسِي طَرْفَةَ عَينٍ وَأَصْلِح شَأْنِي كُلَّهُ لَا إِلَهَ إِلَّا أَنْت

Allahumo rahmataka arjuu falaa takilniy ilaa nafsee torfata a'ynin wa aslah shayin kulluhu la illaha illa anta

Meaning: O Allah, I hope for Your mercy, do not leave me for even the duration of an eye blink (duration) and correct my total condition. Besides You there is none worthy of worship

56. When closing the eyes of the deceased

اللّهمّ اغْفِرْ لِفلاَن (باسمه) وارْفَعْ دَرَجَتَهُ
فِي الْمَهْدِيِّينَ، واخْلُفْهُ فِي عَقِبِهِ فِي
الْغَابِرينَ، واغْفِرْ لَنَا وَلَهُ يَارب الْعَالَمِينَ،
وافْسَحْ لَهُ فِي قَبْرِه ونَوِّر لَهُ فِيه

Allaahumma ighfir li-fulanin (name of the deceased) warfa' darajatahu fil-mahdiyyiina, wakhlufhu fee 'aqibihi fil-ghaabireena , waghfir-lanaa wa lahu yaa Rabbal-'aalameena, waf sah lahu fee qabrihi wa nawwir lahu feehi

Meaning: O Allah, forgive (say the person's name) and raise his place amongst those who are guided. Send him along the path of those who came before, and forgive us and him, O Lord of the worlds. Widen for him his grave and lighten him in it.

57. Supplication for the deceased at the funeral prayer

اللّهُمَّ اغْفِرْ لَهُ وَارْحَمْهُ، وَعَافِهِ، وَاعْفُ عَنْهُ، وَأَكْرِمْ نُزُلَهُ، وَوَسِّعْ مُدْخَلَهُ، وَاغْسِلْهُ بِالْمَاءِ وَالثَّلْجِ وَالْبَرَدِ، وَنَقِّهِ مِنَ الْخَطَايَا كَمَا نَقَّيْتَ الثَّوْبَ الْأَبْيَضَ مِنَ الدَّنَسِ، وَأَبْدِلْهُ دَارًا خَيْرًا مِنْ دَارِهِ، وَأَهْلاً خَيْرًا مِنْ أَهْلِهِ، وَزَوْجًا خَيْرًا مِنْ زَوْجِهِ، وَأَدْخِلْهُ الْجَنَّةَ، وَأَعِذْهُ مِنْ عَذَابِ الْقَبْرِ وَعَذَابِ النَّارِ

Allaahum-maghfir lahu warhamhu, wa 'aafihi, wa'fu 'anhu, wa 'akrim nuzulahu, wa wassi' mudkhalahu, waghsilhu bilmaa'i waththalji walbaradi, wa naqqihi minal-khataayaa kamaa naqqaytath-thawbal-'abyadha minad-danasi, wa 'abdilhu daaran khayran min daarihi, wa 'ahlan khayran min 'ahlihi, wa zawjan khayran min zawjihi, wa 'adkhilhul-jannata, wa. 'a'idhhu min 'adhaabil-qabri wa 'adhaabin-naar.

Meaning: O Allah, forgive him and have mercy on him and give him strength and pardon him. Be generous to him and cause his entrance to be wide and wash him with water and snow and hail. Cleanse him of his transgressions as white cloth is cleansed of stains. Give him an abode better than his home, and a family better than his family and a wife better than his wife. Take him into Paradise and protect him from the punishment of the grave (and from the punishment of Hell-fire).

اللّهُمَّ إن (باسمه) في ذِمَّتِك، وَحَبْلِ جِوَارِك، فَقِهِ مِنْ فِتْنَةِ الْقَبْرِ وَعَذَاب النّار، وَأَنْتَ أَهْلُ الْوَفَاء والْحَقِّ، فَاغْفِرْ لَهُ وارْحَمْهُ، إِنَّكَ أَنْتَ الْغَفُورُ الرّحِيم

Allaahumma 'inna (name the deceased) fee thimmatika, wa habli jiwaarika, faqihi min fitnatil-qabri wa 'athaabinnaari, wa 'Anta 'ahlul-wafaa'i walhaqqi. Faghfir lahu warhaw.hu 'innaka 'Antal-Ghafoorur-Raheem.

O Allah, surely (say the deceased name) is under Your protection, and in the rope of Your security, so save him from the trial of the grave and from the punishment of the Fire. You fulfill promises and grant rights, so forgive him and have mercy on him. Surely You are Most Forgiving, Most Merciful.

58.   Supplication for a deceased child

اللّهُمَّ اجْعَلْهُ فَرَطاً وَذُخْرا لِوالِدَيْهِ، وَشَفِيعاً
مُجَاباً، اللّهُمَّ ثَقِّلْ بِهِ مَوَازِينَهُمَا، وَأَعْظِمْ بِهِ
أُجُورَهُمَا، وَأَلْحِقْهُ بِصَالِحِ الْمُؤْمِنِينَ،
واجْعَلْهُ فِي كَفَالَةِ إِبْرَاهِيمَ، وَقِهِ بِرَحْمَتِكَ
عَذَابَ الْجَحِيمِ، وَأَبْدِلْهُ دَارا خَيْرًا مِنْ دَارِهِ،
وَأَهْلاً خَيْرًا مِنْ أَهْلِهِ، اللّهُمَّ اغْفِرْ لِأَسْلاَفِنَا،
وَأَفْرَاطِنَا، وَمَنْ سَبَقَنَا بِالْإِيمَانِ

Allahumo ij'alahu farato wa dhukran li waalidayhi wa shafee'in mujaaban, Allahumo thaqqil bihi mawaazeenuhu wa a'athamo bihi hujuurahumaa wa-l-hiqhu bi soolihi-l- mumineen, wajalahu fi kafaalati ibroheem waqihi bi rahmatika a'dhaab-l- jaheem, wa abdilhu daaraan khayran min daarihi wa ahlan khayran min ahlihi, Allahummo ighfir liaslaafina, wa afraatina wa man sabaqna-l- eeman

O Allah, make him a precursor, a forerunner and a gem for his parents and an answered intercessor. O Allah, make him weigh heavily in their scales (of good) and multiply their reward. Make him join the righteous of the believers. Place him in the care of Ibrahim. Save him by Your mercy from the punishmentt of Hell. Give him a home better than his home and a family better than his family. O Allah, forgive those who have gone before us, our children lost (by death), and those who have preceded us in Faith

اللّهُمّ أَعِذْه مِنْ عَذاب الْقَبْر

Allahummo a'idhahu min a'dhaabil qabri

Meaning: O Allah protect him from the punishment of the grave

اللّهُمّ اجْعَلْهُ لَنا فَرَطاً، وَسَلَفاً، وأجْرا

Allahumo ij'alahu faraton wa salafan wa ajraa

Meaning: O Allah, make him for us a precursor, a forerunner and a cause of reward

59. Placing the deceased in the grave

بِسْمِ اللّهِ وَعَلَى سُنّةِ رَسُوْلِ اللّهِ

Bismillahu wa a'laa sunnati rasuulullahi

Meaning: With the Name of Allah and according to the Sunnah of the Messenger of Allah

60. Prayers post burial

اللّهُمّ اغْفِرْ لَهُ، اللّهُمّ ثَبِّتْه

Allahumo ighfirlahu, Allahumo thabbithu

Meaning: O Allah him, O Allah give him strength

61. Prayer for grave visitation

السّلاَمَ عَلَيْكُمْ أَهْلَ الدّيَارِ، مِنَ الْمُؤْمِنِينَ وَالْمُسْلِمِيَن، وَإِنّا إِن شَاءَ اللّهُ بِكُمْ لاَحِقُونَ،

وَيَرْحَمُ اللَّهُ الْمُسْتَقْدِمِينَ مِنَّا وَالْمُسْتَأْخِرِينَ

أَسْأَلُ اللَّهَ لَنَا وَلَكُمُ الْعَافِيَة

Assalamu a'laykum ahlad-diyyaar, minal mumineena wa muslimeen wa inna inshallahy bikum laahikun, wa yarhamullahu-l- mustaqdimeen minna-l- musta-akhireen asalullaha lanaa wa lakum-l-a'afiyat

Meaning: Peace be upon you, people of this abode, from among the believers and those who are Muslims, and we, by the Will of Allah, shall be joining you. May Allah have mercy on the first of us and the last of us) I ask Allah to grant us and you strength.

62.   Prayer for condolence visit

إِنَّ لِلَّهِ مَا أَخَذَ، وَلَهُ مَا أَعْطَى وَكُلُّ شَيْءٍ

عِنْدَه بِأَجَلٍ مُسَمًّى فَلْتَصْبِرْ وَلْتَحْتَسِب

Innalillahi maa akhadha wa lahu maa a'atoo wa kullu shayin i'ndahu bii ajlin musamma, fali tasbeer waltahsib

Meaning: Surely, Allah takes what is His, and what He gives is His, and to all things He has appointed a time... so have patience and be rewarded

أَعْظَمَ اللَّهُ أَجْرَكَ، وأَحْسَنَ عَزَاءَ ك وغَفَرَ لِمَيِّتِك

A'athomollahu ajraka wa ahsana a'zaa-aka wa ghafara li mayyitika

Meaning: May Allah magnify your reward, and make perfect your bereavement, and forgive your departed.

63.   Supplication when settling a debt

اللّهُمّ اكْفِنِي بِحَلَالِكَ عَنْ حَرَامِكَ، وأَغْنِنِي بِفَضْلِكَ عَمّنْ سِوَاك

Allaahummak-finee bihalaalika 'an haraamika wa 'aghninee bifadhlika 'amman siwaaka.

Meaning: O Allah, suffice me with what You have allowed instead of what You have forbidden, and make me independent of all others besides You

64.   When the debt is settled

بَارك اللّهُ لَكَ فِي أَهْلِكَ وَمَالِكَ، إنّمَا جَزَاء السّلَفِ الْحَمْدُ والأَداء

Baarakallaahu laka fee 'ahlika wa maalika, 'innamaa jazaa'us-salafil-hamdu wal'adaa'.

Meaning: May Allah bless you in your family and your wealth, surely the reward for a loan is praise and returning (what was borrowed).

CHAPTER 5: EVENING SUPPLICATION AND INVOCATIONS FOR SLEEPING

65. Supplication for evening

اللّهُمَّ مَا أَمْسَ بِي مِنْ نِعْمَةٍ أَوْ بِأَحَدٍ مِنْ

خَلْقِكَ فَمِنْكَ وَحْدَكَ لَا شَرِيكَ لَكَ، فَلَكَ

الْحَمْدُ وَلَكَ الشُّكْرُ

Allahumo maa amsa bii min-ni'matin awbi ahdin min khalqika fa minka wahdak la shareekalak falaka-l- hamdu wa laka shukru

Meaning: O Allah whatever grace has been my share this evening or the share of your creations is from you alone, without a partner, so all praise and thanks is for you

اللّهُمَّ عَافِنِي فِي بَدَنِي، اللّهُمَّ عَافِنِي فِي

سَمْعِي، اللّهُمَّ عَافِنِي فِي بَصَرِي، لاَ إِلَهَ إِلاَّ

أَنْتَ

Allahumo a'afiniy fi badaniy, Allahumo a'afiniy fi sama'ee, Allahumo a'afiniy fi basoree, laaillaha illa anta

Meaning: O Allah grant me health in my body, O' Allah grant me health in my hearing, O' Allah grant me health in my sight, there is no god but you

اللَّهُمَّ إِنِّي أَعُوذُبِكَ مِنَ الْكُفْرِ، والفَقْرِ، .
وأَعُوذُبِكَ مِنْ عَذَاب الْقَبْرِ، لاَ إِلَهَ إِلاّ أَنْت

Allahumo inny a'udhubika minna-l- kufri wal faqri, wa a'udhubika min a'dhaabi-l- qabri, laaillaha illa anta

Meaning: O' Allah I seek refuge with you from disbelieve and poverty, and I seek your protection from the punishment of the grave

بِسْمِ اللَّهِ الَّذِي لاَ يَضُرُّ مَعَ اسْمِهِ شَيْءٌ فِي
الأَرض وَلاَ فِي السَّمَاء وَهُوَ السَّمِيعُ الْعَلِيم

Bismillahi ladhi laa yaduru ma'a ismihi shayun fil ardi wa la fii samai wa huwa samiiun a'leem

Meaning: In the name of Allah, with whose name nothing in the heaven or earth harms, He is the All-hearing and All-knowing

أَمْسَيْنا و امْسَحَ الْمُلْكُ لِلّهِ رب الْعَالَمِينَ، اللّهُمّ إِنِّي أَسْأَلُكَ خَيْرَ هَذَا الْلَيْلِ فَتْحَهُ، وَنَصْرَهُ، وَنُوره وبَرَكَتَهُ، وَهُدَاهُ، وأَعُوذ بِكَ مِنْ شَرّ مَا فِيهِ وشَرّ مَا بَعْدَهَ

Amsayna wa amsaha-l-mukulillahu robbi-l- a'lameen , Allahmo inni as-aluka khayra hadha-l-layl fathahu wa nasorohu wa nuruhu wa barakatuhu wa hudaahu wa a'udhu min sharri ma fihi wa sharri ma ba'dahu

Meaning: We are here this day sovereignty is for Allah the Lord of the Worlds. O" Allah I'm seeking for the goodness of this day its victory, help, light , blessings, guidance. and I seek protection from the evil that is in it and the evil that follows it.

66.   Supplication for sleeping
Recite the following on your palms :

Aayatal Qursiyy

الَلّهُ لَآ إِلَهَ إِلاَّ هُوَ ٱلْحَىُّ ٱلْقَيُّوم لاَ تَأْخُذُهُ
سِنَةٌ وَلاَ نَوْم لَّهُ مَا فِى ٱلسَّمَوَت وما فِى
ٱلْأَرْض مَن ذَا ٱلَّذِى يَشْفَعُ عِندَهُ إِلاَّ بِإِذْنِهِ
يَعْلَمُ مَا بَيْنَ أَيْدِيهِمْ وما خَلْفَهُمْ وَلاَ
يُحِيطُون بِشَىْءٍ مِّنْ عِلْمِهِ إِلاَّ بِمَا شَآءَ وَسِعَ
كُرْسِيُّهُ ٱلسَّمَوَت وٱلْأَرْض وَلاَ يَـُوده
حِفْظُهُمَا وَهُوَ ٱلْعَلِىُّ ٱلْعَظِيم

Allaahu laa 'ilaaha 'illaa Huwal-Hayyul-Qayyuum, laa
ta'khuthuhu sinatunw-wa laa nawm, lahu maa fis-
samaawaati wa maafil- ardi, man thal-lathee yashfa'u
'indahu 'illaa bi'idhnihi, ya'alamu maa bayna 'aydeehim
wa maa khalfahum, wa laa yuheetoona bishay'im-min
'ilmihi 'illaa bimaa shaa'a, wasi'a kursiyyuhus-samaawaati
wal'ardh, wa laa ya'ooduhu hifdhuhumaa, wa Huwal-
'Aliyyul- 'Adheem.

Allah - there is no deity except Him, the Ever-Living, the Sustainer of [all] existence. Neither drowsiness overtakes Him nor sleep. To Him belongs whatever is in the heavens and whatever is on the earth. Who is it that can intercede with Him except by His permission? He knows what is [presently] before them and what will be after them, and they encompass not a thing of His knowledge except for what He wills. His Kursi extends over the heavens and the earth, and their preservation tires Him not. And He is the Most High, the Most Great.

Suratul Ikhlas

بِسْمِ اللّهِ الرّحْمَـٰنِ الرّحِيمِ

قُلْ هُوَ اللّهُ أَحَدٌ، اللّهُ الصّمَدُ، لَمْ يَلِدْ وَلَمْ يُولَدْ، وَلَمْ يَكُنْ لَهُ كُفُوًا أَحَدٌ

Bismi Allahi arrahmani arraheem. Qul huwa Allahu ahad, Allahu assamad, Lam yalid walam yoolad, Walam yakun lahu kufuwan ahad.

Meaning: In the name of Allah the most beneficient, the most merciful.Say 'He is Allah, who is one. Allah, the

73

eternal refuge. He neither begets nor is born. Nor is there to him any equivalent

Suratul Falaq

بِسْمِ اللّٰهِ الرّحْمٰـنِ الرّحِيمِ

قُلْ أَعُوذ بِرَبِّ الْفَلَقِ، مِن شَرّ مَا خَلَقَ، وَمِن شَرّ غَاسِقٍ إِذا وَقَبَ، وَمِن شَرّ النّفّاثَات فِي الْعُقَدِ، وَمِن شَرّ حَاسِدٍ إِذا حَسَدَ

Bismillahi arrahmani arraheem. Qul a'aoothu birabbi alfalaq, Min sharri ma khalaq, Wamin sharri ghasiqin ithawaqab, Wamin sharri annaffathatifee al'uqad, Wamin sharri hasidin itha hasad

Meaning: In the name of Allah the most beneficient, the most merciful

Say ' I seek refuge in the lord of the day break. From the evil of that which he created. And from the evil of darkness when it settles. And from the evil of the blower in knots. And from the evil of the envier when he envies.

Suratul Nas

بِسْمِ اللّهِ الرّحْمٰنِ الرّحِيمِ.

قُلْ أَعُوذ بِرَبِّ النّاسِ، مَلِكِ النّاسِ، إِلَٰهِ النّاسِ، مِن شَرّ الْوَسْوَاس الْخَنّاسِ، الّذِي يُوَسْوِس فِي صُدُور النّاسِ، مِنَ الْجِنّةِ وَالنّاسِ.

Bismi Allahi arrahmani arraheem. Qul a'aoothu birabbi annas, Maliki annas, Ilahi annas, Min sharri alwaswasi alkhannas, Allathee yuwaswisu fee sudoori annas, Mina aljinnati wannas.

Meaning: In the name of Allah the most beneficent, the most merciful

Say ' I seek refuge in the Lord of mankind. The Sovereign of mankind. The God of mankind. From the evil of the retreating whisperer. Who whispers evil into the breast of mankind. From amongst the Jinn and mankind.

Other supplications

بِاسْمِكَ رَبِّي وَضَعْتُ جَنْبِي، وَبِكَ أَرْفَعُهُ،
فَإِن أَمْسَكْتَ نَفْسِي فَارْحَمْهَا، وإِن أَرْسَلْتَهَا
فَاحْفَظْهَا، بِمَا تَحْفَظُ بِهِ عِبَادك الصَّالِحِين

Bismika robbi wado'at jambee, wabika arfa'uhu, fa in amsakta nafsee farhamhaa wa in arsaltaha fahfath-haa bimaa tahfathu bihi i'baadaka-sooliheen

Meaning: In Your Name my Lord, I lay myself down and with Your Name I rise. And if my soul You take, have mercy on it, and if You send it back then protect it as You protect Your pious slaves.

اللَّهُمَّ بِاسْمِكَ أَمُوت وأَحْيَا

Allahumo bismika aamutu wa ahya

Meaning: O Allah, in your name I die and I live

اللّهُمّ إِنّك خَلَقْت نَفْسِي وأَنْت تَوَفّاهَا، لَك مَمَاتُهَا ومَحْيَاهَا، إِن أَحْيَيْتَهَا فَاحْفَظْهَا، وإِن أَمَتّهَا فَاغْفِرْ لَهَا، اللّهُمّ إِنّي أَسْأَلُك الْعَافِيَة

Allahumo innaka khalaqta nafsee wa anta tawaffaahaa laka mamaatuhaa inahyaatahaa wa in amatahaa faghfirliha, Allahumo inni asaluka-l-a'fiyat

Meaning: O Allah, You have created my soul and You take it back. Unto You is its death and its life. If You give it life then protect it, and if You cause it to die then forgive it. O Allah, I ask You for strength

67. Invocation against unrest or fear while sleeping

أَعُوذ بِكَلِمَاتِ اللّهِ التّامّاتِ مِنْ غَضَبِهِ وعِقابِهِ، وَشَرّ عِبَادهِ، وَمِنْ هَمَزَاتِ الشّيَاطِينِ وأَن يَحْضُرُون

A'udhubi kalimaati min godabihi wa i'qabihi wa sharri i'baadihi wa min hamazaati shayaateen wa an yahduroon

Meaning: I seek refuge in the Perfect Words of Allah from His anger and His punishment, from the evil of His slaves and from the taunts of devils and from their presence

CHAPTER 6: OTHER DAILY SUPPLICATION

68.   Upon sneezing

الْحَمْدُ لله

Alhamdulillahi

Meaning: All praise is due to Allah

After the one nearby replies, Say:

يَهْدِيكُمُ اللّه وَيُصْلِحُ بَالَكُمْ

Yahdeekumu llahu wa yuslihi baalakum

Meaning: May Allah guide you and set your affairs in order

69.   Supplication on hearing someone sneeze

مُكَاللّٰهِيَرْح

Yarhamka llahi

Meaning: May the mecry of Allah be on you

Supplication after the reply

70.   Invocation when happy

سُبْحَانَاللّٰه

Subhanallahi

Meaning: Glory be to Allah

71.   Invocation when angry

أَعُوذ بِاللّٰهِ مِنَ الشَّيْطَان الرّجِيم

A'udhubillahi minas-shaytooni rajeem

Meaning: I seek refuge with Allah from the accursed devil

72. Supplication on seeing a Muslim

السَّلَام عَلَيْكُمْ ورَحْمَةُ اللهِ وَبَرَكَاتُه

As-salamu alaykum warahmotullahi wabarakatuhu

Meaning: May the peace and blessings of Allah be upon you

73. Returning the salaam

وَعَلَيْهِ السَّلَام ورَحْمَةُ اللّه وبَرَكَاتُه

Wa a'layhis- salaam wa rahmatullahi wabarakatuhu

Meaning: May the mercy and blessings of Allah be upon you too

74. Supplication when at a sitting or gathering

رب اغْفِرْ لِي وَتُبْ عَلَيَّ إِنَّكَ أَنْتَ التَّوَّاب الْغَفُور

Robbi ighfirly wa tub- a'layya innaka antat-tawwabu lghafuur

Meaning: My Lord, forgive me and accept my repentance, You are the Ever-Relenting, the All-Forgiving

75. Supplication for when it rains

اللّهُمّ صَيِّباً نَافِعا

Allahumo soohiban nafia'n

Meaning: O' Allah bring beneficial clouds

76. Supplication during windstorm

اللّهُمّ إِنِّي أَسْأَلُكَ خَيْرَها، وأَعُوذ بِكَ مِنْ شَرَّهَا

81

Allahumo inni asaluka khayraha wa a'udhubika min sharriha

Meaning: O' Allah I am asking for the good in this and protect me from the evil in it

77. Supplication upon receiving a pleasant news

الْحَمْدُ لِلّه

Alhamdulillahi

Meaning: All praise is due to Allah

78. Supplication for a lost item

اللّهُمّ راد الضّالّة وَهادي الضّالّة أنْت تَهْدِي مِنَ الضّلالَة اردد عَلَيّ ضَالّتِي بِقُدْرَتِك وَسُلْطَانِك فَإِنّهَا مِنْ عَطَائِك وَفَضْلِك

Allahumo raadda daal-lati wa haadii daal-lati anta tahdee mina- daalati irdud a'layya daal-lati biqudratika wa sultoonika fa innaha min a'tooika wa fadlika

Meaning: "O Allah, the One who returns the lost, by Your power and awe return what I have lost, for surely I have received it as Your gift and favor

79.   Supplication before sexual intercourse

بِسْمِ اللّهِ، اللّهُمّ جَنِّبْنَا الشّيْطَانَ، وَجَنِّبِ الشّيْطَانَ مَا رَزَقْتَنَا

Bismillahi Allahummo jannibna ashayton wa jannibi-shayton maa razaqtanaa

Meaning: With the Name of Allah. O Allah, keep the Devil away from us and keep the Devil away from that which You provide for us

CHAPTER 6 SUPPLICATION FROM THE QURAN

1 Al-Baqarah 2:127

رَبّنَا تَقبّل مِنّاْ إِنّكَ
أَنتَ السّمِيعُ الْعَلِيم ـ

Rabbana taqabbal minna innaka anta sami'un a'leem

Meaning: "Our Lord, accept [this] from us. Indeed You are the Hearing, the Knowing.

2 Al-Baqarah 2:201

" رَبّنَاۤ ءاتِنَا فِى ٱلدّنْيَا حَسَنَةً وَفِى ٱلءاخِرَة
"حَسَنَةً وَقِنَا عَذاب ٱلنّار

Rabbana aatina fi dunya hasanatan wa fil-akhirati hasanatan wa qina a'dhaaban-naar

Meaning: Our Lord, give us in this world [that which is] good and in the Hereafter [that which is] good and protect us from the punishment of the Fire."

3   Al-Baqarah 2:286

رَبَّنَا لَا تُؤَاخِذْنَا إِن نَّسِينَا أَوْ أَخْطَأْنَا رَبَّنَا وَلَا تَحْمِلْ عَلَيْنَا إِصْرًا كَمَا حَمَلْتَهُ عَلَى ٱلَّذِينَ مِن قَبْلِنَا رَبَّنَا وَلَا تُحَمِّلْنَا مَا لَا طَاقَةَ لَنَا بِهِ وَٱعْفُ عَنَّا وَٱغْفِرْ لَنَا وَٱرْحَمْنَا أَنتَ مَوْلَىٰنَا فَٱنصُرْنَا عَلَى ٱلْقَوْمِ ٱلْكَٰفِرِينَ

Rabbana laa tu akhidhna inna siina aw akhtona, Rabbana wa la tuhammil a'layna isran kama hamaltahu a'la ladhina min qablina, Rabbana wa la tuhammil maalaa tooqota lana bihi wa 'afuanna waghfirlana warhamna anta mawlaana fansurna a'la-l- qawmi-l- kaafireen

Meaning: "Our Lord, do not impose blame upon us if we have forgotten or erred. Our Lord, and lay not upon us a burden like that which You laid upon those before us. Our Lord, and burden us not with that which we have no ability to bear. And pardon us; and forgive us; and have mercy upon us. You are our protector, so give us victory over the disbelieving people."

4 Aal-e-Imran 3:8

$$رَبَّنَا لاَ تُزِغْ قُلُوبَنَا بَعْدَ إِذ هَدَيْتَنَا وَهَبْ لَنَا$$

$$مِن لَّدُنكَ رَحْمَةً إِنَّكَ أَنتَ الْوَهَّاب$$

Rabbana la tudhi qulubana b'ada idh hadaytana wa hablana min ladun karahmatan innaka anta-l- wahab

Meaning: "Our Lord, let not our hearts deviate after You have guided us and grant us from Yourself mercy. Indeed, You are the Bestower".

5 Aal-e-Imran 3:9

رَبَّنَا إِنَّكَ جَامِعُ النَّاسِ لِيَوْمٍ لاَّ رَيْبَ فِيهِ
إِنَّ اللهَ لاَ يُخْلِفُ الْمِيعَادَ

Rabbana innak jaamiun lin-nasi laa rayba fihi innallaha laa yukhlifu-l-mi'aad

Meaning: Our Lord, surely You will gather the people for a Day about which there is no doubt. Indeed, Allah does not fail in His promise."

6   Aal-e-Imran 3:16

رَبَّنَا إِنَّنَا آمَنَّا فَاغْفِرْ لَنَا ذُنُوبَنَا وَقِنَا عَذَابَ
النَّارِ

Rabbana innana aamanna faghfirlana dhunubana waqina a'dhaaban- naar

Meaning: "Our Lord, indeed we have believed, so forgive us our sins and protect us from the punishment of the Fire,"

7   Aal-e-Imran 3:53

رَبَّنَا آمَنَّا بِمَا أَنزَلْتَ وَاتَّبَعْنَا الرَّسُولَ فَاكْتُبْنَا

مَعَ الشَّاهِدِينَ

Rabbana aamana bima anzalta wataba'ar- rasul faktubna ma'ashaahideen

Meaning: "Our Lord, we have believed in what You revealed and have followed the messenger Jesus, so register us among the witnesses [to truth]."

8   Aal-e-Imran 3:147

رَبَّنَا اغْفِرْ لَنَا ذُنُوبَنَا وَإِسْرَافَنَا فِي أَمْرِنَا

وَثَبِّتْ أَقْدَامَنَا وَانصُرْنَا عَلَى الْقَوْمِ الْكَافِرِينَ

Rabbana ighfirlana dhunubana wa israafana fi amrina wa thabbit aqdaamana fansurna a'la-l- qawmil-kaafireen

Meaning: "Our Lord, forgive us our sins and the excess [committed] in our affairs and plant firmly our feet and give us victory over the disbelieving people."

9   Aal-e-Imran 3:191

رَبَّنَا مَا خَلَقْتَ هَذَا بَاطِلاً سُبْحَانَكَ فَقِنَا

عَذَابَ النَّار -

Rabanna maa khalaqta hadha baatilan subhanaka faqinna a'dhaban naar

Meaning: "Our Lord, You did not create this aimlessly; exalted are You [above such a thing]; then protect us from the punishment of the Fire".

10   Aal-e-Imran 3:192

رَبَّنَا إِنَّكَ مَن تُدْخِلِ النَّارَ فَقَدْ أَخْزَيْتَهُ وَمَا

لِلظَّالِمِينَ مِنْ أَنصَارَ

Rabanna innaka man tudkhilin-naara faqad akhdhayta, wa maa lidhaalimeena min ansaar

Meaning: "Our Lord, indeed whoever You admit to the Fire - You have disgraced him, and for the wrongdoers there are no helpers".

12   Aal-e-Imran 3:193

رَبَّنَا إِنَّنَا سَمِعْنَا مُنَادِياً يُنَادِي لِلإِيمَانِ أَنْ

آمِنُوا بِرَبِّكُمْ فَآمَنَّا رَبَّنَا فَاغْفِرْ لَنَا ذُنُوبَنَا

وَكَفِّرْ عَنَّا سَيِّئَاتِنَا وَتَوَفَّنَا مَعَ الأَبْرَارِ

Rabanna innana sam'ina munadiyyan- yunadii lil-eeman an aaminu birabikum fa aamanna. Rabanna faghfirlan dhunubana wa kaffir'anna sayyiaatina wa tawwafanna ma'l-abrar

Meaning: "Our Lord, indeed we have heard a caller calling to faith, [saying], 'Believe in your Lord,' and we have believed. Our Lord, so forgive us our sins and remove from us our misdeeds and cause us to die with the righteous".

13   Aal-e-Imran 3:194

رَبَّنَا وَآتِنَا مَا وَعَدتَّنَا عَلَىٰ رُسُلِكَ وَلَا تُخْزِنَا يَوْمَ الْقِيَامَةِ ۗ إِنَّكَ لَا تُخْلِفُ الْمِيعَادَ

Rabanna aatina maa wa'adt-tana a'la rusulika wa la tukhdhina yawma-l- qiyamat innaka la tukhlifu-l- mi'aad

Meaning: "Our Lord, and grant us what You promised us through Your messengers and do not disgrace us on the Day of Resurrection. Indeed, You do not fail in [Your] promise."

14   Al-Ma'idah 5:83

رَبَّنَا آمَنَّا فَاكْتُبْنَا مَعَ الشَّاهِدِينَ

Rabanna aamanna faktubna ma'ashahideen

Meaning: "Our Lord, we have believed, so register us among the witnesses".

15 Al-Ma'idah 5:114

رَبَّنَا أَنزِل عَلَيْنَا مَائِدَةَ مِنَ السَّمَاءِ تَكُونُ لَنَا
عِيداً لأَوَّلِنَا وَآخِرِنَا وَآيَةً مِّنكَ وَارزُقْنَا
وَأَنتَ خَيْرُ الرَّازِقِينَ

Rabanna anzil a'layna maaidatan minnas- samai takuunu lana i'dan li awwalina wa akhirna wa aayatan minka warzukna wa anta khayrur- raziqeen

Meaning: "O Allah, our Lord, send down to us a table [spread with food] from the heaven to be for us a festival for the first of us and the last of us and a sign from You. And provide for us, and You are the best of providers."

16 Al-A'raf 7:23

رَبَّنَا ظَلَمْنَا أَنفُسَنَا وَإِن لَّمْ تَغْفِرْ لَنَا وَتَرْحَمْنَا
لَنَكُونَنَّ مِنَ الْخَاسِرِينَ

Rabanna thallamna anfusana wa inl-lam taghfirlana wa tarhamna lanakunanna minna-l- khasireen

Meaning: "Our Lord, we have wronged ourselves, and if You do not forgive us and have mercy upon us, we will surely be among the losers."

17   Al-A'raf 7:47

رَبَّنَا لاَ تَجْعَلْنَا مَعَ الْقَوْمِ الظَّالِمِين

Rabanna la taja'lna ma'al qawmi dhalimeen

Meaning: "Our Lord, do not place us with the wrongdoing people."

18   Al-A'raf 7:89

رَبَّنَا افْتَحْ بَيْنَنَا وَبَيْنَ قَوْمِنَا بِالْحَقِّ وأنتَ خَيْرُ الْفَاتِحِين

Rabanna iftah baynana wa bayna qawmina   bil-haqi wa anta khayrul- fatiheen

Meaning: "Our Lord, decide between us and our people in truth, and You are the best of those who give decision."

19   Al-A'raf 7:126

رَبَّنَا أَفْرِغْ عَلَيْنَا صَبْراً وَتَوَفَّنَا مُسْلِمِينِ

Rabanna afrig a'layna sobran wa tawafanna muslimeen

Meaning: "Our Lord, pour upon us patience and let us die as Muslims [in submission to You]."

20   Yunus 10:85-86

فَقَالُوا عَلَى اللّهِ تَوَكَّلْنَا رَبَّنَا لاَ تَجْعَلْنَا فِتْنَةً لِّلْقَوْمِ الظَّالِمِينَ و وَنَجِّنَا بِرَحْمَتِكَ مِنَ الْقَوْمِ الْكَافِرِينَ

Rabanna la taja'lna fitnatan li qawmit- tholimeen wa najjina bi rahmatika minal qawmil- kaafireen

Meaning: "Our Lord, make us not [objects of] trial for the wrongdoing people And save us by Your mercy from the disbelieving people."

21 Ibrahim 14:38

رَبَّنَا إِنَّكَ تَعْلَمُ مَا نُخْفِي وَمَا نُعْلِنُ وَمَا يَخْفَىٰ عَلَى اللّهِ مِن شَيْءٍ فِي الْأَرْضِ وَلَا فِي السَّمَاءِ

Rabanna innaka ta'lam ma nokhfi wa ma nu'lin wa ma yakhfa a'lallahi shayan fil-ardi wala fi samai

Meaning: "Our Lord, indeed You know what we conceal and what we declare, and nothing is hidden from Allah on the earth or in the heaven."

22 Ibrahim 14:40

95

رب اجْعَلْنِي مُقِيمَ الصَّلاَةَ وَمِن ذُرِّيَّتِي رَبَّنَا
وتقبّلْ دُعَاء

Rabanna ija'lni muqeema solaati wa min dhuriyyati rabanna taqabbal dua'

Meaning: "My Lord, make me an establisher of prayer, and [many] from my descendants. Our Lord, and accept my supplication".

23 Ibrahim 14:41

رَبَّنَا اغْفِرْ لِي وَلِوَالِدَي وَلِلْمُؤْمِنِين يَوْم
يَقُوم الْحِسَاب

Rabanna ighfirly wali waalidayya walili mumineena yawma yaqumul- hisaab

Meaning: "Our Lord, forgive me and my parents and the believers the Day the account is established."

24   Al-Kahf 18:10

رَبَّنَا آتِنَا مِن لَّدُنكَ رَحْمَةً وَهَيِّئْ لَنَا مِنْ
أَمْرِنَا رَشَدًا

Rabanna aatina min ladunka rahmatan wa hayyilana min amrina rashadan

Meaning: "Our Lord, grant us from Yourself mercy and prepare for us from our affair right guidance."

25   Ta-Ha 20:45

رَبَّنَا إِنَّنَا نَخَافُ أَن يَفْرُطَ عَلَيْنَا أَوْ أَن يَطْغَىٰ

Rabanna innakna nakhaafu an-yafrutu a'laynaa aw an yatga

Meaning:, "Our Lord, indeed we are afraid that he will hasten [punishment] against us or that he will transgress."

26   Al-Mu'minun 23:109

رَبَّنَا آمَنَّا فَاغْفِرْ لَنَا وَارْحَمْنَا وأنت خَيْرُ
الرَّاحِمِين

Rabanna aamanna faghfirlana war-hamna wa anta khayru raahimeen

Meaning: "Indeed, there was a party of My servants who said, 'Our Lord, we have believed, so forgive us and have mercy upon us, and You are the best of the merciful."

27   Al-Furqan 25:65-66

رَبَّنَا اصْرِف عَنَّا عَذَابَ جَهَنَّمَ إِن عَذَابَهَا
كَان غَرَام إِنَّهَا سَآءَت مُسْتَقَرًّا وَمُقَامًا

Rabanna isrifanna a'dhaba jahannam inna a'dhaabaha kaana goraama, innaha saa at mustaqarran wa muqaama

Meaning: "Our Lord, avert from us the punishment of Hell. Indeed, its punishment is ever adhering   Indeed, it is evil as a settlement and residence."

28   Al-Furqan 25:74

رَبَّنَا هَبْ لَنَا مِنْ أزواجِنَا وذرِيّاتِنَا قُرَّةَ أعْيُنٍ
واجْعَلْنَا لِلْمُتَّقِينَ إمَامًا

Rabanna hablana min azwaajina wa dhurriyyatina qurrata a'yunin waja'lna lilmutaqeena imaama

Meaning: "Our Lord, grant us from among our wives and offspring comfort to our eyes and make us an example for the righteous."

29   Ghafir 40:7

رَبَّنَا وَسِعْت كُلَّ شَيْءٍ رَّحْمَةً وَعِلْمًا فَاغْفِرْ
لِلّذِينَ تَابُوا واتّبَعُوا سَبِيلَكَ وَقِهِمْ عَذَابْ
الْجَحِيم

Rabbana wasi'at kulla shayin rahmatan wa i'lman faghfir lilladhina taabu wat-taba'u sabiilika waqihim a'dhaba-l-jaheem

Meaning: "Our Lord, You have encompassed all things in mercy and knowledge, so forgive those who have repented and followed Your way and protect them from the punishment of Hellfire.

30   Ghafir 40:8-9

رَبَّنَا وأدْخِلْهُمْ جَنَّاتِ عدْنِ الَّتِي وعدتّهُمْ

ومَن صَلَحَ مِنْ آبَائِهِمْ وأزواجِهِمْ وذرِّيَاتِهِمْ

إِنَّكَ أَنتَ الْعَزِيزُ الْحَكِيمُ وَقِهِمُ السَّيِّئَات

ومَن تَقِ السَّيِّئَات يَوْمَئِذٍ فَقَدْ رَحِمْتَهُ وذَلِكَ

هُوَ الْفَوْزُ الْعَظِيمِ

Rabbana wa adkhilihim jannaati a'dnin- llati wa'ad tahum wa man solaha wa min aaba ihim wa azwaajihim wa dhurriyatihim innaka antal- azeezu-l-hakeem wa qihim sayyiat wa man taqi sayyiat yawma idhinfaqad rahimtah wa zaalika huwal- fawzu-l- azeem

Meaning: "Our Lord, and admit them to gardens of perpetual residence which You have promised them and whoever was righteous among their fathers, their spouses and their offspring. Indeed, it is You who is the Exalted in Might, the Wise. And protect them from the evil consequences [of their deeds]. And he whom You protect from evil consequences that Day - You will have given him mercy. And that is the great attainment."

31   Al-Hashr 59:10

رَبَّنَا اغْفِرْ لَنَا ولإخْوانِنَا الّذِينَ سَبَقُوْنَا بِالإِيمَان ولَا تَجْعَلْ فِي قُلُوبِنَا غِلاً لِّلَّذِينَ آمَنُوا رَبَّنَا إِنّكَ رءوف رَّحِيم

Rabbana ighfirlana wali ikwaanina sabakuuna bili eeman wala taja'l fi quluubina gillan lilladhina aamanu, robbana innak raufur- raheem

Meaning: "Our Lord, forgive us and our brothers who preceded us in faith and put not in our hearts [any] resentment toward those who have believed. Our Lord, indeed You are Kind and Merciful."

101

32 Al-Mumtahanah 60:4

رَّبَّنَا عَلَيْكَ تَوَكَّلْنَا وَإِلَيْكَ أَنَبْنَا وَإِلَيْكَ الْمَصِيرُ.

Rabbana a'layka tawakkalina wa ilayka anabna wa ilaykal-maseer

 Meaning: "Our Lord, upon You we have relied, and to You we have returned, and to You is the destination."

33 Al-Mumtahanah 60:5

رَبَّنَا لاَ تَجْعَلْنَا فِتْنَةً لِّلَّذِينَ كَفَرُوا وَاغْفِرْ لَنَا رَبَّنَا إِنَّكَ أَنتَ الْعَزِيزُ الْحَكِيمُ

Rabanna la taj'alna fitnatan lilladhina kafaru waghfirlana rabbana innaka anta-l- a'zeezu-l- hakeem

Meaning: "Our Lord, make us not [objects of] torment for the disbelievers and forgive us, our Lord. Indeed, it is You who is the Exalted in Might, the Wise."

34   At-Tahrim 66:8

رَبَّنَا أَتْمِمْ لَنَا نُورَنَا وَاغْفِرْ لَنَا إِنَّكَ عَلَىٰ كُلِّ شَيْءٍ قَدِيرٌ

Rabbana at mimlana nuurana waghfirlana innaka a'la kulli shayin qadeer

Meaning: "Our Lord, perfect for us our light and forgive us. Indeed, You are over all things competent."

REFERENCES

☐ Quran - Sahih International Trandlation English

☐ Sahih Bukhari by Imam Bukhari

☐ Sahih Muslim by Muslim bin Hajjaj

☐ Sunan Al Sughra by Al-Nasai

☐ Sunan Abu Dawood by Abu Dawood

☐ Jami-I- Tirmidhi by Al- Tirmidhi

Made in the USA
Middletown, DE
16 September 2024

60960872R00064